Let's Explore Mexico

by Walt K. Moon

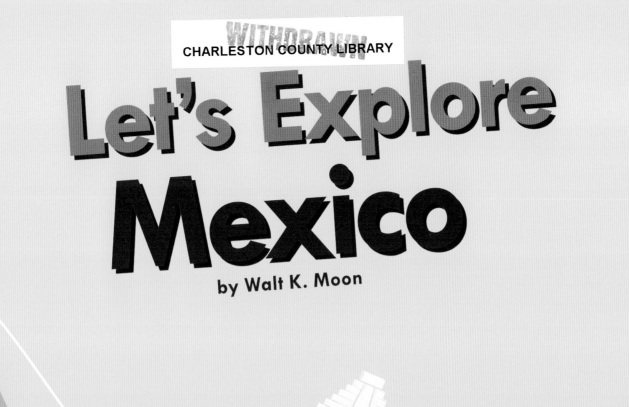

BUMBA BOOKS™

LERNER PUBLICATIONS ◆ MINNEAPOLIS

Note to Educators:

Throughout this book, you'll find critical thinking questions. These can be used to engage young readers in thinking critically about the topic and in using the text and photos to do so.

Lerner Publications Company
A division of Lerner Publishing Group, Inc.
241 First Avenue North
Minneapolis, MN 55401 USA
For reading levels and more information, look up this title at www.lernerbooks.com.

Library of Congress Cataloging-in-Publication Data

Names: Moon, Walt K., author.
Title: Let's explore Mexico / by Walt K. Moon.
Description: Minneapolis : Lerner Publishing Group, Inc., 2017. | Series: Bumba books™ — Let's explore countries | Includes bibliographical references and index. | Audience: Grades K–3; Ages 4–8.
Identifiers: LCCN 2016018690 (print) | LCCN 2016022498 (ebook) | ISBN 9781512430059 (lb : alk. paper) | ISBN 9781512430219 (pb) | ISBN 9781512430233 (eb pdf)
Subjects: LCSH: Mexico—Juvenile literature.
Classification: LCC F1208.5 .M66 2017 (print) | LCC F1208.5 (ebook) | DDC 972—dc23

LC record available at https://lccn.loc.gov/2016018690

Manufactured in the United States of America
1 – VP – 12/31/16

Expand learning beyond the printed book. Download free, complementary educational resources for this book from our website, www.lerneresource.com.

Table of Contents

A Visit to Mexico

Mexico is a country

in North America.

It is south of the

United States.

4

Mexico has big deserts.

It has rain forests.

It has tall volcanoes.

It lies between

two oceans.

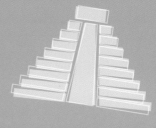

Jaguars live in the rain forests.

Snakes live in the deserts.

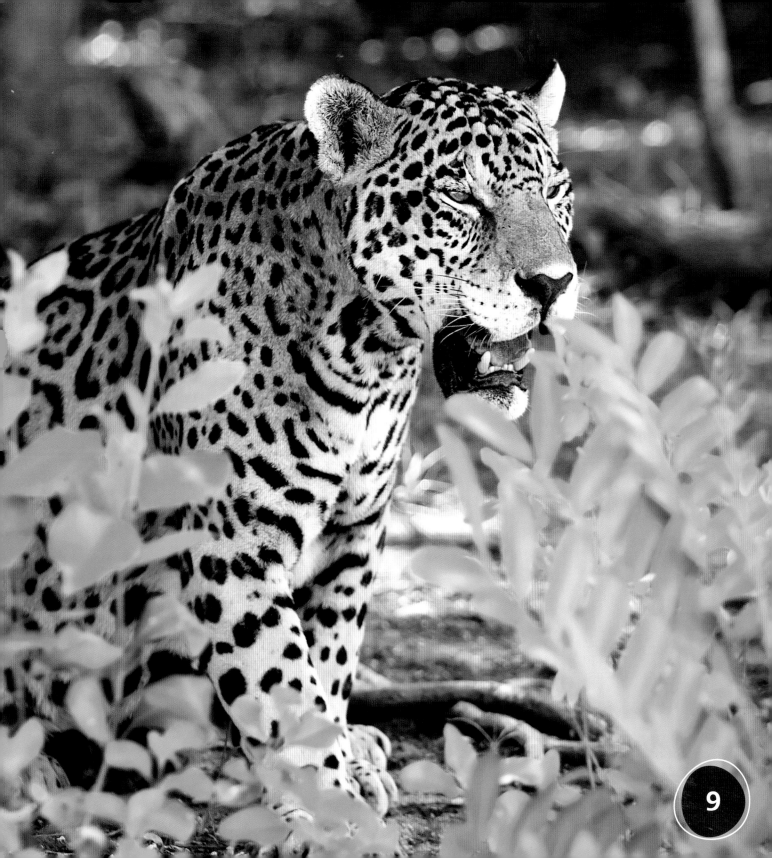

Cactuses grow in the deserts.

These plants store water.

They have sharp points.

What else might live in the desert?

Most Mexican people live in cities.

Others live in small villages.

How might village life be different from city life?

13

Mexico has a long history.
Some buildings have
stood for hundreds
of years.
These buildings were
once part of cities.

What do you think happened to this city?

Mexican food is popular around

the world.

Many people eat tacos.

Mexican food can be spicy.

Soccer is the top sport in Mexico.

Baseball is popular too.

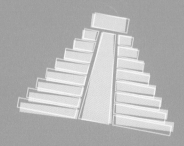

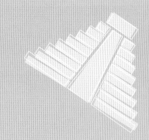

People like to

visit Mexico.

They go to the beaches.

They swim or play

in the sand.

Would you like to go

to Mexico?

Map of Mexico

deserts

Mexico

rain forests

oceans

volcanoes

Picture Glossary

cactuses

desert plants with sharp points on them

deserts

dry places that get little rain

jaguars

big cats with spotted fur

volcanoes

mountains that make lava and gases

23

Index

Read More

McDonnell, Ginger. *Next Stop: Mexico.* Huntington Beach, CA: Teacher Created Materials, 2012.

Perkins, Chloe. *Living in . . . Mexico.* New York: Simon Spotlight, 2016.

Robinson, Joanna J. *Mexico.* Mankato, MN: Child's World, 2015.

Photo Credits

The images in this book are used with the permission of: © ChameleonsEye/Shutterstock.com, pp. 4–5; © Kuryanovich_Tatsiana/Shutterstock.com, pp. 6–7, 23 (bottom right); © Patryk Kosmider/Shutterstock.com, pp. 9, 23 (bottom left); © Leonardo Gonzalez/Shutterstock.com, pp. 10, 23 (top left); © abalcazar/iStock.com, p. 13; © Anna Omelchenko/Shutterstock.com, pp. 14–15; © Ricardo Villasenor/Shutterstock.com, p. 16; © Natursports/Shutterstock.com, p. 19; © BlueOrange Studio/Shutterstock.com, pp. 20–21; © Red Line Editorial, p. 22; © Carrie Merrell/iStock.com, p. 23 (top right).

Front Cover: © LRCImagery/iStock.com.